W9-CRS-233

LIFE'S LITTLE
TREASURE BOOK

On Parenting

H. JACKSON BROWN, JR.

RUTLEDGE HILL PRESS®

· NASHVILLE, TENNESSEE

Published in Nashville, Tennessee, by Rutledge Hill Press,
Inc., 211 Seventh Avenue North, Nashville, Tennessee
37219. Distributed in Canada by H. B. Fenn and Company,
Ltd., 34 Nixon Road, Bolton, Ontario L7E 1W2. Distributed
in Australia by The Five Mile Press Pty., Ltd., 22 Summit
Road, Noble Park, Victoria 3174. Distributed in New
Zealand by Tandem Press, 2 Rugby Road, Birkenhead,
Auckland 10. Distributed in the United Kingdom by
Verulam Publishing, Ltd., 152a Park Street Lane, Park Street,
St. Albans, Hertfordshire AL2 2AU.

Typography by Compass Communications, Inc.,
Nashville, Tennessee
Illustrations by Greg King
Floral Illustrations by Cristine Mortensen
Book design by Harriette Bateman

ISBN: 1-55853-330-3

Printed in Mexico
4 5 6 7 8 9 — 01 00 99 98

INTRODUCTION

$\mathcal{W}$e have to have a license to drive a car, to carry a gun, even to go fishing. But there's no qualification for parenthood beyond biology. There's not even a required reading list.

Fortunately, parents have allies in the formidable task of child rearing—teachers, coaches, church leaders, friends, and extended family members. But we should remember that it's in the home that children best learn self-discipline, courage, compassion, and responsibility—the tools that help them to become men and women of strong and admirable character. My father used to say that a parent's good example is the best sermon. He was right.

Good parenting is not easy. And it's never mistake free. Our children will try our patience, test our endurance, and even when they're not around, they preoccupy our hearts and minds. I've known for a long time that to be the parent I want to be, I need reminding of what I should be thinking and doing. The entries in this book have encouraged me with instruction, inspiration, and when nothing else worked, a little laughter. I hope you find them useful, too.

The habits we form
from childhood
make all
the difference.

—Aristotle

*P*lant a tree the day
your child is born.

∾

*R*emember the three universal
healers: Calamine lotion,
warm oatmeal, and hugs.

∾

*K*iss your children goodnight,
even if they are already asleep.

$\mathcal{R}$emember that the word
discipline means "to teach."

&

$\mathcal{C}$hoose a pediatrician who
is a parent.

&

$\mathcal{B}$e prompt when picking up
or dropping off
your children for school
or other activities.

$\mathcal{I}$'ve learned that . . .

even though I don't show it,
I'm so glad my parents love
each other so much.

—Age 16

I get a lump in my throat every
time I think of the day when
my daughter will marry.

—Age 44

*C*ompliment the parent
when you observe a
well-behaved child.

❧

*U*ntil your children move out
of your house, don't buy
anything suede.

❧

*P*ut a lock on your
bedroom door.

Don't be afraid to be boss.
Children are constantly
testing, attempting to see
how much they can get
away with—how far you
will let them go—
and they secretly hope you
will not let them go too far.

—Ann Landers

Remember that misbehavior
is often a child's way of
saying, "Show me that
you love me."

Let your children overhear
you saying nice things about
them to other adults.

Read to your children.

∽

Listen to your children.

∽

Pray with your children.

$\mathcal{D}$on't let your kids convince
you that a balanced meal is a
Big Mac in both hands.

∾

$\mathcal{I}$f you want your children
to turn out well, spend
twice as much time with them
and half as much money.

When no great harm will result, let your children do it their way even if you know they are wrong. We learn more from our mistakes than from our successes.

I've learned that . . .

I still like it when my mom checks in my room before she goes to bed.   —Age 17

I would rather be told what I'm doing right than what I'm doing wrong.

—Age 13

Nothing speaks
more loudly to
a child than
a good parent's
quiet example.

Find something to praise in
your child every day.

∿

Consider this equation:
the amount of time you spend
with your children while they
are growing up equals the
amount of time they will spend
with you while you are
growing old.

$\mathcal{D}$on't brag about one of your children in the presence of another.

∿

$\mathcal{T}$each your children respect for teachers and police officers.

∿

$\mathcal{R}$equire your children to do their share of the household chores.

$\mathcal{E}$ach year, take a first-day-of-school photograph of your children.

❧

$\mathcal{T}$*he most beautiful sight*
you will ever see is
your child running to you
with outstretched arms.

$\mathcal{D}$on't ever be too busy to give your children a hug and a kiss.

∾

$\mathcal{N}$ever begin a conversation with a child with, "You always . . ."

∾

$\mathcal{T}$each your children the pride, satisfaction, and dignity of any job done well.

I've learned that . . .

my father saved me from
many a foolish act with these
words, "go ask your Mother."

—Age 26

you're asking for trouble when
you leave a three-year-old in
the car with the keys in the
ignition.

—Age 33

$\mathcal{A}$lways tell family members you love them before they go away for a few days.

∾

$\mathcal{H}$old a child's hand when crossing the street.

∾

$\mathcal{A}$lways be the first parent to jump into the pool with the kids. They'll love you for it.

*In every child who is born,
under no matter what
circumstances, and of no
matter what parents,
the potentiality of the
human race is born again.*

—James Agee

$\mathcal{D}$on't decide anything when you are angry.

❧

$\mathcal{K}$eep your promises.

❧

$\mathcal{N}$ever say anything uncomplimentary about your spouse in the presence of your children.

No matter how old a mother is, she watches her middle-aged children for signs of improvement.

—Florida Scott Maxwell

*B*efore I got married I had six theories about bringing up children; now, I have six children and no theories.

—John Wilmont, Earl of Rochester

$\mathcal{G}$et to know your
child's teachers.

❧

$\mathcal{A}$ttend your children's school
plays and athletic contests.

❧

$\mathcal{N}$ever watch a movie in front
of your children involving
activities you don't want
them doing.

Children in a family are like flowers in a bouquet; there's always one determined to face in an opposite direction from the way the arranger desires.

—Anonymous

Never give a child a drum.

❧

Let your children pick out
their own lunch boxes.

❧

The persons hardest to convince
they're at the retirement age
are children at bedtime.

—Shannon Fife

$\mathcal{I}$nsanity is
hereditary;
you get it from
your children.

—Sam Levenson

I've learned that . . .

no matter what their ages
or how far away they may be,
you never stop wanting to
keep a protective arm around
your children.   —Age 67

it's hard to lie when you are
looking into your mom's eyes.

—Age 9

*H*elp your child plant a
small garden.

❧

*E*ncourage your children to get
involved with scouting.

❧

*R*eally listen to your children.
Let them know that you
understand and empathize
with their feelings.

There are three ways to get something done: do it yourself, hire someone, or forbid your kids to do it.

—Monta Crane

*T*reat your children with the same respect you want them to give you.

❧

*A*cknowledge even small improvements.

❧

*D*on't overschedule your child's extracurricular activities.

$\mathcal{G}$ive your young children the opportunity to be a part of your family's decision-making process; they will surprise you.

❧

$\mathcal{P}$ut up a basketball goal in the driveway.

❧

$\mathcal{E}$ncourage all children over five to have a library card.

The most positive
thing you can do
for your children
is to improve
your marriage.

*A*lways acknowledge
your child's wounds,
no matter how slight.

❧

*D*on't make eating everything
on their plate an issue
with children.

❧

*A*llow your children to face the
consequences of their actions.

Don't take up a man's time
talking about the smartness
of your children; he wants
to talk to you about the
smartness of his own children.

—Ed Howe

❧

Here all mankind is equal:
rich and poor alike.
They love their children.

—Euripides

I've learned that . . .

if either of your parents are mad, don't—and I repeat don't—ask for money.

—Age 10

the love that accompanies the birth of a child exceeds your greatest expectation. —Age 27

Treasure your children for what they are, not for what you want them to be.

Spend twice as much time
praising as you do criticizing.

❧

Make the rules for your
children clear, fair,
and consistent.

❧

Encourage your children
to join a choir.

Teach your children the value
of money, the importance of
saving, and the joy of giving.

⌘

Remind your children that
regardless of what happens,
you'll always be there
for them.

*N*ever miss an opportunity to take your child fishing.

❧

*L*earn CPR.

❧

*L*earn the Heimlich maneuver.

Likely as not, the child
you can do the least with
will do the most
to make you proud.

—Mignon McLaughlin

Cleaning your house while
your kids are still growing
Is like shoveling the walk
before it stops snowing.

—Phyllis Diller

$\mathcal{I}$'ve learned that . . .

no matter where you are in
the house your mom can hear
you. —Age 13

when your five-year-old lies
down on the couch, she's
sick. —Age 37

Take a holiday
family photograph each year
in the same spot, such as
by a favorite tree in your yard.
In years to come,
you'll have a wonderful
record of the growth of
your family, as well as
the growth of the tree.

$\mathcal{T}$ell your kids often how terrific they are and that you trust them.

∾

$\mathcal{K}$now who your children's friends are.

∾

$\mathcal{S}$ave the newspapers from the day your children were born.

$\mathcal{D}$on't give in to whining
demands and tantrums.

∾

$\mathcal{S}$et limits on the amount and
content of the television your
children watch.

∾

$\mathcal{D}$on't pick up after your
children. That's their job.

*Y*ou can never know
how much your
parents loved you
until you become
a parent yourself.

$\mathcal{D}$on't allow children to ride in the back of a pickup truck.

❧

$\mathcal{D}$isplay a piece of art created by your child where you can see it every day.

❧

$\mathcal{L}$et your children be children. Don't push them into adulthood.

*A*fter children argue and
have said the "I'm sorry's,"
ask each one to say something
nice about the other.

❧

*R*emember that no parent ever
convinced her child to eat
something by saying,
"It's good for you."

*N*ever criticize your children
for calling home collect.

∾

*V*olunteer to be a
Little League umpire.

∾

*T*each your sons
as well as your daughters
to cook.

$\mathcal{I}$ve learned that . . .

there's nothing sweeter than sleeping with your babies and feeling their breath on your cheeks.　　　　—Age 38

when my child gets upset, he calms down much sooner if I stay calm.　　　　—Age 33

*R*emember that
the more a
child feels valued,
the better his
values will be.

Oh, to be only half as wonderful as my child thought I was when he was small, and only half as stupid as my teenager now thinks I am.

—Rebecca Richards

Never tell a young person that something cannot be done. God may have been waiting for centuries for somebody ignorant enough of the impossibility to do that thing.

—Dr. J. A. Holmes

$\mathcal{D}$evelop a secret
family sign that says,
"I love you."

☙

$\mathcal{W}$hen children want to talk
to you, turn off the TV or put
down what you're reading
and give them your
undivided attention.

Reserve a door jamb to record the birthday heights of your children. Never paint it.

∾

Share with your child the inspiring and instructive stories and poems in William Bennett's *The Book of Virtues* (Simon & Schuster).

Check a baby sitter's references carefully before hiring him or her.

❧

Attend church with your children.

❧

Always keep a couple of Wet-Naps in the glove box.

I've learned that . . .

my grown children remember
and treasure the things we did
rather than what was bought.

—Age 65

the moment my pregnancy
test was positive, I became
my mother.   — Age 21

When I was a boy of fourteen, my father was so ignorant I could hardly stand to have the old man around. But when I got to be twenty-one, I was astonished at how much he had learned in seven years.

—Mark Twain

Teach your children what
to do in case your
house catches fire.

❧

Give your child
swimming lessons
at an early age.

❧

Never say "shut up"
to a child.

*R*emember that
your words can deeply hurt.

∽

*R*emember that
your words can quickly heal.

∽

*L*eave notes in unexpected
places that tell your child how
much he or she is loved.

You have a wonderful child.
Then, when he's thirteen,
gremlins carry him away
and leave in his place a
stranger who gives you not
a moment's peace.

—Jill Eikenberry

*A*ccept your child's
right to privacy.

❧

*V*olunteer as a family to
work in a soup kitchen or
homeless shelter during
the holidays.

❧

*A*lways blow a kiss when
driving away from loved ones.

Remember, if your
teenager doesn't think
you are a real embarrassment
and a hard-nosed bore,
you are probably not
doing your job.

∞

Never break off
communications with
your children no matter
what they do.

Be consistent.

❧

Be fair.

❧

Be forgiving.

Spoil your
spouse, not
your children.

Pretty much all the honest truth telling there is in the world today is done by children.

—Oliver Wendell Holmes

Every beetle is a gazelle in the eyes of its mother.

—Moorish Proverb

I've learned that . . .

when you think your children haven't learned a thing you've taught them, they will surprise you by saying or doing something that proves they really did! —Age 45

it really doesn't hurt a child to go to bed without a bath.

—Age 32

$\mathcal{L}$et your children help
you work, even if it
slows you down.

❧

$\mathcal{N}$ever assume something is
childproof. A three-year-old
could put Houdini to shame.

❧

$\mathcal{A}$sk a blessing
before each meal.

When you make a mistake,
admit it quickly and apologize.

❧

Don't allow your children or
grandchildren to call you
by your first name.

❧

Every once in a while,
let your kids play in the rain.

*L*ive so that
when your children
think of fairness,
caring, and integrity,
they think of you.

When the best in the world
visits your town for a concert,
exhibition, or speech,
take the family to see it.

∾

Before your children get their
driver's licenses, teach them
how to jack up a car safely
and change a tire.

When greeting adults and your child is with you, introduce her to them.

❧

Teach your children that "just because I said so" is an acceptable parental answer.

❧

Start the standing ovation at the end of school plays.

I've learned that . . .

you should never bug your
parents when they are paying
bills or preparing taxes.

—Age 11

children sleep better if they
have had a hug and a kiss from
both Mom and Dad. —Age 60

*F*orget the broccoli and the
Brussels sprouts.

∾

*R*emember the milk
and cookies.

∾

*T*each your children
never to underestimate
someone with a disability.

Children have never been very good at listening to their elders, but they have never failed to imitate them.

—James Baldwin

*H*ug your children after
you discipline them.

∿

*N*ever go near a kid with a
water hose unless you want
to get wet.

∿

*E*ncourage your children
to learn to play
a musical instrument.

*A*ssemble a baby bed
in the room where it will be
used. If you don't,
you'll discover it's too big
to get through the door.

∾

*L*et your children observe
your being generous to
those in need.

Take your teenager with you
when you buy a car or
expensive household item and
let them learn from
the experience.

$\mathcal{I}$'ve learned that . . .

the best compliment my
children gave me was that
they wished they could have
a marriage like my husband's
and mine.

—Age 72

I'm getting more and more
like my mom and I'm kind of
happy about it.   —Age 19

Enjoy at least one meal a day
when the entire family
is in attendance.

∞

Criticize the behavior,
not the child.

∞

Teach your child that
when she divides anything,
the other kid gets first pick.

$\mathcal{R}$esist comparing
your children to their
siblings or other children.

∾

$\mathcal{S}$end valentines to your
children as well as your spouse.

∾

$\mathcal{L}$earn the rules of any sport
your children play.

$\mathcal{W}$hen all else fails,
console yourself
by saying,
"It's just a phase."

$\mathcal{G}$o on family vacations and take lots of pictures.

❧

$\mathcal{C}$onvince your children that your love is not based on their performance.

❧

$\mathcal{F}$rame anything your child brings home on his first day of school.

I've learned that . . .

when you ask your mom a question and she says "no," always go ask your dad.

—Age 13

children need a lot more smiles and hugs than lectures and instructions.

—Age 48

It's this way with children.
It's cumulative.
The more you love them,
the more you sacrifice;
and the more
you sacrifice, the more
you love.

—William Graham Summer

*J*udge your success as
a parent to the degree that
your children feel safe,
wanted, and loved.

*S*et aside your dreams for your
children and help them attain
their own dreams.

$\mathcal{Y}$our family

is

your treasure.